fairy cakes

fairy cakes

hamlyn

NOTES

Medium eggs have been used throughout.

A few recipes include nuts or nut derivatives. It is advisable for those with known allergic reactions to nuts and nut derivatives and those who may be potentially vulnerable to these allergies, such as pregnant and nursing mothers, invalids, the elderly, babies and children, to avoid dishes made with nuts and nut oils. It is also prudent to check the labels of prepared ingredients for the possible inclusion of nut derivatives.

Ovens should be preheated to the specified temperature. If using a convection oven, follow the manufacturer's instructions for adjusting the time and temperature.

First published in Great Britain in 2004 by Hamlyn,
a division of Octopus Publishing Group Ltd
2–4 Heron Quays, London E14 4JP

Copyright © Octopus Publishing Group Ltd 2004

ISBN 0 600 60963 4

A CIP catalogue record for this book is available from the British Library

Printed and bound in China

10 9 8 7 6 5 4 3

contents

introduction

Home-made cakes are always popular with family and friends, and fairy cakes are no exception. Not only are they tasty and incredibly quick and easy to make, they also give you plenty of scope for decorating. They make ideal novelty cakes for kids' parties but are equally suitable for grown-up parties and for special family occasions like Christmas, Easter and Mother's Day.

Fairy cakes keep well so you can make them in advance and keep a handy supply in the freezer or an airtight container until they're needed. If you really don't have time to make any you can even buy plain, undecorated fairy cakes and decorate them yourself – within half an hour you can have a batch of beautifully presented cakes ready for guests or a hungry family.

Types of icing

Glacé icing The simplest glacé icing is made just with icing sugar and water beaten into a smooth icing. Alternatives include the use of orange or lemon juice instead of water, the addition of flavourings like instant coffee powder, or the use of food colouring to tint the icing. Use a thin glacé icing to coat the top of cakes, or add more icing sugar for a stiffer consistency and use it for decorative piping.

Buttercream The simplest recipe requires just icing sugar and butter. Like glacé icing, it can be coloured and/or flavoured with ingredients such as cocoa or instant coffee powder, lemon curd or finely grated citrus rind and can be used both for coating the tops of fairy cakes and for decorative piping. It is very simple to make but can also be bought ready-made.

Rolled fondant This soft and smooth, easy-to-use commercial icing is available from cake decorating suppliers and some supermarkets. It usually comes in white, with a subtle flavour, but like the other icings can be easily coloured or flavoured by kneading it with food colouring or flavouring extracts. Rolled fondant can be rolled out and cut into flat shapes or moulded into fun 3D novelty decorations to put on top of cakes. Knead the rolled fondant before use to warm it up, then roll it out on a surface dusted with icing sugar and move it around frequently to keep it from sticking.

Writing icing Another ready-to-use commercial icing, writing icing comes in tubes with changeable tips for piping. Ideal for fun and speedy cake decorating, it is available in a variety of colours.

Decorating fairy cakes
Decorating any cake is fun, but working with fairy cakes is particularly satisfying since you can produce impressive results in virtually no time at all. The various home-made or commercial icings suitable for fairy cakes can be coloured and used for topping the cakes, for decorative piping, or for modelling figures, but don't think such decorations restrict fairy cakes to children. You can just as easily decorate fairy cakes for special occasions like weddings (see page 32), or create cakes for a special afternoon tea party using whipped cream and thick custard as cake toppings instead of icing – see Espresso Cream Cakes (see page 58), Strawberry Cream Cakes (see page 52) and Praline Custard Cakes (see page 55).

There are a few decorating accessories and ingredients that you will find useful if you intend to do a lot of fairy cakes decorating, although you may already have some items at home.

Piping bags and tips You can buy reusable nylon piping bags and large plastic 'syringes', both of which can be used with changeable tips. However, it is probably easier to use disposable paper piping bags for small-scale decorating. These can be bought ready made from good cake decorating suppliers or you can easily make your own from triangles of greaseproof

paper. The advantage of disposable piping bags is that you can have several bags of icing in use at one time, whereas if you have only one reusable piping bag you will have to wash it out each time you want to change the colour or type of icing you are using. The two most useful tips for decorating fairy cakes are the star tip, used for fancy lines and star shapes, and the plain tip, used for lines, dots and scribbling. Metal tips give better results than plastic ones.

Cookie cutters Made of metal or plastic, cookie cutters are invaluable for cutting out rolled fondant. They come in a variety of shapes – from simple round cutters to numerical and alphabetical shapes, animals, cars, hearts, stars, teddy bears and flowers, among many others. If you cannot find a cutter with the motif that you want, simply cut out the fondant freehand with a small sharp knife. Instead of a round pastry cutter you can use an upturned glass to cut out circles.

Food colouring Food colouring is available in liquid, gel and paste forms, and in many colours, although you can buy a few basic colours and mix them yourself to create other shades. They are quite concentrated so you need only a drop or two to colour icing. Transfer the colour to the icing on the end of a cocktail stick and mix well after each addition so that the colour is evenly distributed throughout, with no streaks. You can always add more colouring but it is difficult to rectify a case of over-colouring that results in an offputting blood red or navy blue icing!

Edible cake decorations Besides the huge range of small sweets suitable for decorating fairy cakes – such as candy-coated chocolate drops, chocolate buttons, mini Easter eggs, wine gums and jelly beans – there are specialist edible decorations for cakes. Edible silver or gold balls, known as dragees, are small sugar balls with a coating of edible silver or gold leaf, while sugar strands are available in different sizes and various colours and flavours. Other specialist products include rice paper flowers and chocolate and coloured sprinkles. You can also buy chocolate curls or make your own by paring off 'ribbons' from a bar of softened chocolate with a vegetable peeler.

150 g (5 oz) **unsalted butter** or **margarine**, softened

150 g (5 oz) **caster sugar**

175 g (6 oz) **self-raising flour**

3 **eggs**

1 teaspoon **vanilla extract**

Vanilla fairy cakes

1 Line a 12-section bun tray with paper cake cases. Put all the cake ingredients in a mixing bowl and beat with a hand-held electric whisk for 1–2 minutes until light and creamy. Divide the mixture evenly among the cake cases.

2 Bake in a preheated oven, 180°C (350°F), Gas Mark 4, for 18–20 minutes until risen and just firm to the touch. Transfer to a wire rack to cool.

Makes 12
Preparation time: 10 minutes
Cooking time: 18–20 minutes

VARIATIONS
Chocolate:
Substitute 15 g (½ oz) cocoa powder for 15 g (½ oz) of the flour.
Chocolate Chip:
Add 50 g (2 oz) plain, milk or white chocolate chips.
Coffee:
Add 1 tablespoon espresso or strong coffee powder.
Lemon/Orange/Citrus:
Add the finely grated rind of 1 lemon or 1 small orange, or combine the rinds of ½ lemon and ½ orange.
Cranberry or Blueberry:
Add 75 g (3 oz) dried cranberries or blueberries, chopped if large.
Ginger:
Add 2 teaspoons ground ginger and use light muscovado sugar instead of caster sugar.
Sultana:
Add 75 g (3 oz) sultanas.

Carrot fairy cakes

1 Line a 12-section bun tray with paper cake cases. Put the butter, sugar, flour, baking powder, mixed spice, ground almonds, eggs and orange rind in a mixing bowl and beat with a hand-held electric whisk for 1–2 minutes until light and creamy.

2 Add the grated carrots and sultanas and stir in until evenly combined. Divide the mixture evenly among the cake cases.

3 Bake in a preheated oven, 180°C (350°F), Gas Mark 4, for 25 minutes until risen and just firm to the touch. Leave to cool in the bun tray.

Makes 12
Preparation time: 15 minutes
Cooking time: 25 minutes

VARIATION
Banana:
Replace the grated carrots and orange rind with 1 large banana, mashed until smooth.

125 g (4 oz) **unsalted butter** or **margarine**, softened

125 g (4 oz) **light muscovado sugar**

150 g (5 oz) **self-raising flour**

1 teaspoon **baking powder**

1 teaspoon **ground mixed spice**

75 g (3 oz) **ground almonds**

2 **eggs**

finely grated rind of ½ **orange**

150 g (5 oz) **carrots**, grated

50 g (2 oz) **sultanas**

Fruit and nut fairy cakes

150 g (5 oz) **unsalted butter** or **margarine**, softened

150 g (5 oz) **light muscovado sugar**

200 g (7 oz) **self-raising flour**

3 **eggs**

1 teaspoon **almond extract**

50 g (2 oz) **chopped mixed nuts**

75 g (3 oz) **mixed dried fruit**

1 Line a 12-section bun tray with paper cake cases. Put the butter, sugar, flour, eggs and almond extract in a mixing bowl and beat with a hand-held electric whisk for 1–2 minutes until light and creamy.

2 Add the chopped nuts and dried fruit and stir in until evenly combined. Divide the mixture evenly among the cake cases.

3 Bake in a preheated oven, 180°C (350°F), Gas Mark 4, for 25 minutes until risen and just firm to the touch. Transfer to a wire rack to cool.

Makes 12
Preparation time: 10 minutes
Cooking time: 25 minutes

Buttercream

1 Put the butter and icing sugar in a bowl and beat well with a wooden spoon or hand-held electric whisk until smooth and creamy.

2 Add the vanilla extract and hot water and beat again until smooth.

Makes enough to cover 12 fairy cakes
Preparation time: 5 minutes

VARIATIONS
Chocolate:
Mix 2 tablespoons cocoa powder with 2 tablespoons boiling water and use instead of the vanilla extract and hot water.
Citrus:
Add the finely grated rind of 1 orange or lemon.

150 g (5 oz) **unsalted butter**, softened

250 g (8 oz) **icing sugar**

1 teaspoon **vanilla extract**

2 teaspoons **hot water**

Cream cheese frosting

1 Beat the cream cheese in a bowl until smooth and creamy. Add the icing sugar and lemon juice and beat until completely smooth.

Makes enough to cover 12 fairy cakes
Preparation time: 5 minutes

125 g (4 oz) **cream cheese**

175 g (6 oz) **icing sugar**

1 tablespoon **lemon juice**

100 g (3½ oz) **plain** or **milk chocolate**, chopped

2 tablespoons **milk**

50 g (2 oz) **unsalted butter**

75 g (3 oz) **icing sugar**

Chocolate fudge frosting

1 Put the chocolate, milk and butter in a small, heavy-based saucepan and heat gently, stirring until the chocolate and butter have melted.

2 Remove from the heat and stir in the icing sugar until smooth. Spread the frosting over the tops of fairy cakes while still warm.

Makes enough to cover 12 fairy cakes
Preparation time: 5 minutes

200 g (7 oz) **white chocolate**, chopped

5 tablespoons **milk**

175 g (6 oz) **icing sugar**

White chocolate fudge frosting

1 Put the chocolate and milk in a heatproof bowl, set over a saucepan of gently simmering water and leave until melted, stirring frequently.

2 Remove the bowl from the pan and stir in the icing sugar until smooth. Spread the frosting over the tops of fairy cakes while still warm.

Makes enough to cover 12 fairy cakes
Preparation time: 5 minutes

2 tablespoons **strawberry** or **raspberry jam**

12 **fairy cakes** (see pages 10–12)

175 g (6 oz) **green ready-to-roll icing**

icing sugar, for dusting

4 **flaked chocolate bars**, cut into 5 cm (2 inch) lengths

50 g (2 oz) **red ready-to-roll icing**

50 g (2 oz) **yellow ready-to-roll icing**

50 g (2 oz) **white ready-to-roll icing**

25 g (1 oz) **black ready-to-roll icing**

Snakes in the jungle

As long as you have green icing for the cake bases, you can make the snakes in any colours you like. Orange can easily be made by blending red and yellow icing, and pink by blending red and white.

1 Using a pastry brush, brush jam over the top of each fairy cake. Knead the green ready-to-roll icing on a surface lightly dusted with icing sugar. Roll out very thinly and cut out 12 circles using a 6 cm (2½ inch) round cookie cutter. Place a green circle on top of each cake.

2 To shape a snake, take a small ball of ready-to-roll icing – about 7 g (¼ oz) – and roll under the palm of the hand to a thin sausage about 12–15 cm (5–6 inches) long, tapering it to a point at one end and shaping a head at the other. Flatten the head slightly and mark a mouth with a small, sharp knife.

3 Thinly roll a little ready-to-roll icing in a contrasting colour and cut out small diamond shapes. Secure along the snake using a dampened paintbrush. Wrap the snake around a length of flaked chocolate and position on top of a cake.

4 Make more snakes in the same way, kneading small amounts of the coloured ready-to-roll icing together to make different colours. For some of the cakes, press the chocolate bar vertically into the cake.

5 To make the snakes' eyes, roll small balls of white icing and press tiny balls of black icing over them. Secure to the snakes' heads with a dampened paintbrush.

Makes 12
Decoration time: 45 minutes

2 tablespoons **raspberry** or **strawberry jam**

12 **fairy cakes** (see pages 10–12)

175 g (6 oz) **red ready-to-roll icing**

icing sugar, for dusting

125 g (4 oz) **black ready-to-roll icing**

15 g (½ oz) **white ready-to-roll icing**

small piece of **candied orange peel**, cut into matchstick lengths

Ladybirds

Thin strips of candied orange peel are used for the antennae on these little bugs. If you cannot get candied orange peel use small chocolate sticks instead.

1 Using a pastry brush, brush jam over the top of each fairy cake. Knead the red ready-to-roll icing on a surface lightly dusted with icing sugar. Roll out very thinly and cut out 12 circles using a 6 cm (2½ inch) round cookie cutter. Place a red circle on top of each cake.

2 Roll out thin strips of black ready-to-roll icing and position one across each red circle, securing with a dampened paintbrush. Roll out half the remaining black icing to a thin sausage shape, about 1 cm (½ inch) in diameter. Cut into very thin slices and secure to the cakes to represent ladybird spots.

3 From the remaining black icing make oval-shaped heads and secure in position. Roll small balls of the white ready-to-roll icing for eyes and press tiny balls of black icing over them. Secure with a dampened paintbrush.

4 To make the ladybirds' antennae, press the lengths of candied orange peel into position behind the heads, pressing small balls of black icing on to their ends. Use tiny pieces of white icing to shape smiling mouths.

Makes 12
Decoration time: 30 minutes

Sea monster

1 Divide the buttercream between 2 bowls. Colour one half with the blue food colouring and the other with the green. Using a small palette knife, swirl the blue buttercream over a large flat platter or tray.

2 Remove one cake from its paper case and slice off the base at an angle so the top of the cake can be arranged over another at an angle to make the monster's face.

3 Spread the green buttercream over the tops of the 11 cakes in their cases. Place the cut cake on top of one of them and spread this with buttercream, too. Arrange the cakes on the blue buttercream base in a snaking line with the 'face' cake at the front.

4 Knead the green ready-to-roll icing on a surface lightly dusted with icing sugar. Roll out 125 g (4 oz) of the icing, keeping the rest wrapped in clingfilm, and cut out

circles using a 7 cm (3 inch) round cookie cutter. Cut the circles in half and position each semicircle, upright, on the 9 centre cakes. Use a little more icing to shape a small pointed tail and secure to the cake at the end.

5 For the legs, divide the reserved green icing into 4 pieces. Shape each into a sausage, flatten the end and cut out claw shapes. Secure around the cakes, bending them so the claws face forward.

6 Roll the green icing trimmings and a little red icing together until marbled. Shape horns and secure to the monster's head. Position the sweets for eyes, then finish the eyes and add a mouth with a little black ready-to-roll icing.

Makes 1 'monster' cake of 12 fairy cakes
Decoration time: 20 minutes

1 quantity **Buttercream** (see page 13)

blue and **green food colourings**

12 **fairy cakes** (see pages 10–12)

375 g (12 oz) **green ready-to-roll icing**

icing sugar, for dusting

15 g (½ oz) **red ready-to-roll icing**

2 red 'dots' **gumdrops**

15 g (½ oz) **black ready-to-roll icing**

½ quantity **Buttercream** (see page 13)

12 **fairy cakes** (see pages 10–12)

100 g (3½ oz) **brown ready-to-roll icing**

icing sugar, for dusting

100 g (3½ oz) **yellow ready-to-roll icing**

100 g (3½ oz) **pink ready-to-roll icing**

15 g (½ oz) **white ready-to-roll icing**

15 g (½ oz) **black ready-to-roll icing**

black food colouring

On the farm

1 Using a palette knife, spread a thick layer of the buttercream over 4 of the cakes and lightly peak. Spread the rest of the buttercream over the remaining cakes.

2 To make the sheep, take 75 g (3 oz) of the brown ready-to-roll icing, wrapping the remainder in clingfilm. Knead the icing on a surface lightly dusted with icing sugar. Reserve a small piece for the ears and roll the remainder into 4 balls. Flatten each ball into an oval shape and gently press on to the cakes thickly spread with buttercream. Shape and position small ears on each sheep.

3 To make the cows, reserve a small piece of the yellow ready-to-roll icing for the ears. Roll the remainder into 4 balls and flatten into oval shapes as large as the cake tops. Gently press on to 4 more cakes. Shape and position the ears. Use the remaining brown ready-to-roll icing to shape the cows' nostrils and horns, securing with a dampened paintbrush.

4 To make the pigs, reserve 25 g (1 oz) of the pink ready-to-roll icing for the snouts and ears. Roll the remainder into 4 balls and flatten into rounds, almost as large as each cake top. Shape and position the snouts and floppy ears, pressing 2 small holes in each snout with the tip of a cocktail stick or fine skewer.

5 Use the white and black icing to make all the animals' eyes – their shape and size to suit each animal. Roll small balls of white icing and press tiny balls of black icing over them. Secure with a dampened paintbrush.

6 Use a fine paintbrush, dipped in the black food colouring, to paint on additional features.

Makes 12
Decoration time: 45 minutes

1 quantity **Buttercream** (see page 13)

blue food colouring

12 **fairy cakes** (see pages 10–12)

25 g (1 oz) **blue ready-to-roll icing**

25 g (1 oz) **red ready-to-roll icing**

25 g (1 oz) **green ready-to-roll icing**

50 g (2 oz) **yellow ready-to-roll icing**

icing sugar, for dusting

50 g (2 oz) **white ready-to-roll icing**

Rainbow cakes

1 Colour the buttercream with the blue food colouring and spread it all over the tops of the fairy cakes using a small palette knife.

2 To make the rainbows, take 15 g (½ oz) of the blue, red, green and yellow icing and roll each piece under the palms of the hands on a surface lightly dusted with icing sugar until about 40 cm (16 inches) long. Push the strips together and then lightly roll with a rolling pin to flatten them and secure together.

3 Cut into 6 pieces, roughly 7 cm (3 inches) long, and secure to half the cakes, bending them into rainbow shapes and trimming off any excess around the edges. Reserve 25 g (1 oz) of the remaining yellow icing, then use all the leftover coloured icing to make another 6 rainbows for the rest of the cakes in the same way.

4 Thinly roll out the white icing and cut out little clouds. Secure to half the cakes.

5 To make the sun, thinly roll the remaining yellow icing and cut out 6 x 4 cm (1½ inch) circles. Using the tip of a sharp knife cut out little triangles from around the edges to make points. Bend the points slightly to one side and position the suns on the remaining cakes.

Makes 12
Decoration time: 25 minutes

Princess cakes

If you can find them, use silver-coloured paper cake cases to make these little fairy cakes even more fit for a princess.

1 quantity **Buttercream** (see page 13)

pink food colouring

12 **fairy cakes** (see pages 10–12)

edible silver balls

1 Divide the buttercream between 2 bowls and add a few drops of pink food colouring to one bowl. Mix well to colour the buttercream. Using a small palette knife, spread the pink buttercream over the tops of the fairy cakes to within 5 mm (¼ inch) of the edges, doming it up slightly in the centre.

2 Put half the white buttercream in a piping bag fitted with a writing nozzle and the remainder in a bag fitted with a star nozzle. Pipe lines, 1 cm (½ inch) apart, across the pink buttercream, then across in the other direction to make a diamond pattern.

3 Use the icing in the other bag to pipe little stars around the edges. Decorate the piped lines with silver balls.

Makes 12
Decoration time: 20 minutes

1 quantity **Buttercream** (see page 13)

green or **yellow food colouring**

12 **fairy cakes** (see pages 10–12)

175 g (6 oz) **white ready-to-roll icing**

icing sugar, for dusting

50 g (2 oz) **red ready-to-roll icing**

50 g (2 oz) **blue ready-to-roll icing**

coloured **sugar strands**

Number cakes

These are quick and easy and a great party cake for younger children. You can cut out the numbers by hand using a sharp knife, or use small number cookie cutters. The numbers could simply run from 1 to 12, or could represent the ages of the party goers.

1 Colour the buttercream with green or yellow food colouring and spread all over the tops of the fairy cakes using a small palette knife.

2 Knead the white ready-to-roll icing on a surface lightly dusted with icing sugar then roll out. Cut out 12 circles using a 6 cm (2½ inch) round cookie cutter and gently press one on to the top of each cake.

3 Roll out the red ready-to-roll icing and cut out half the numbers. Secure to the cakes with a dampened paintbrush. Use the blue ready-to-roll icing for the remaining numbers.

4 Lightly brush the edges of white icing with a dampened paintbrush and scatter over the sugar strands.

Makes 12
Decoration time: 15 minutes

1 quantity **Cream Cheese Frosting** (see page 13)

12 **Carrot Fairy Cakes** (see page 11)

15 g (½ oz) **white ready-to-roll icing**

75 g (3 oz) **red ready-to-roll icing**

handful of **small multi-coloured sweets**

icing sugar, for dusting

1 tube **green writing icing**

fine red **ribbon**, to decorate (optional)

Christmas stockings

Use any selection of the smallest sweets you can find to decorate these little cakes. Alternatively, use larger, soft sweets and chop them into small pieces. If you are making them for small children you might prefer to use Vanilla Fairy Cakes (see page 10) and spread them with Buttercream (see page 13).

1 Using a small palette knife, spread the frosting over the tops of the fairy cakes, spreading it right to the edges.

2 Roll the white ready-to-roll icing and a tiny piece of the red ready-to-roll icing together on a work surface under your fingers so they twist together. Cut into 2 cm (¾ inch) lengths and bend one end of each length to make candy canes. You'll need about 24 altogether.

3 Pile several coloured sweets to one side on the top of each cake and tuck the candy canes among them.

4 Knead the remaining red icing on a surface lightly dusted with icing sugar. Roll out then cut out small stocking shapes using a sharp knife, making sure the top edge of each stocking is at least 2.5 cm (1 inch) wide. Lay the stocking shapes just over the sweet decorations. Use the green writing icing to pipe details on to the stockings.

5 If liked, tie a length of red ribbon around each paper cake case to decorate and finish with a bow.

Makes 12
Decoration time: 20 minutes

Christmas garland

Make the cakes a couple of days beforehand, or well in advance and freeze them, so all you have to do is assemble the garland up to 24 hours before serving. Use gold, silver, patterned or white paper cake cases.

1 Press the jam through a sieve into a small saucepan and add the water. Heat gently until softened then spread in a thin layer over the tops of the fairy cakes.

2 Arrange 15–16 of the cakes in a staggered circle on a round flat platter or tray, at least 35 cm (14 inches) in diameter. Using a small fine sieve or tea strainer dust the cakes on the platter with plenty of icing sugar.

3 Fold a piece of paper into 4 thicknesses then cut out a holly leaf shape, about 6 cm (2½ inches) long. Press a holly leaf paper template gently on the centre of 4 more cakes and dust lavishly with icing sugar. Carefully lift off the templates by sliding a knife under the paper to remove them without disturbing the icing sugar. Repeat on the remaining cakes. Arrange the cakes in a circle on top of the first layer.

4 Cut the grapes into small clusters. Tuck all the fruits into the gaps around the cakes and into the centre of the plate. Finish by arranging small sprigs of bay leaves around the fruits.

Makes 1 garland of 24 fairy cakes
Decoration time: 15 minutes

6 tablespoons **apricot jam**

1 tablespoon **water**

24 **Fruit and Nut Fairy Cakes** (see page 12) or **Cranberry Fairy Cakes** (see page 10)

icing sugar, for dusting

bunch of **red grapes**, washed

bunch of **green grapes**, washed

3–4 **clementines**, halved

3–4 **figs**, halved

plenty of **bay leaf sprigs**

100 g (3½ oz) **white ready-to-roll icing**

200 g (7 oz) **icing sugar**, plus extra for dusting

12 **fairy cakes** (see pages 10–12)

½ quantity **Buttercream** (see page 13)

4–5 teaspoons **cold water**

25 g (1 oz) **desiccated coconut**

Christmas stars

These festive cakes look stunning on the Christmas tea table. If you have time, make the stars at least 2 hours in advance so they have firmed up before you decorate the cakes.

1 Knead the white ready-to-roll icing on a surface lightly dusted with icing sugar. Roll out thickly and cut out star shapes using a small star-shaped cookie cutter. Transfer to a baking sheet lined with nonstick baking parchment and leave to harden while decorating the cakes.

2 Using a small sharp knife, cut out a deep, cone-shaped centre from each cake. Fill the cavity in each cake with buttercream and position a cut-out cone on each with the crust side face down.

3 Mix the icing sugar in a bowl with the cold water until smooth – the icing should hold its shape but not be too firm. Carefully spread the icing over the cakes and scatter with desiccated coconut.

4 Gently press a star into the top of each cake and leave to set.

Makes 12
Decoration time: 25 minutes

12 **Fruit and Nut Fairy Cakes**
(see page 12)

4 tablespoons **brandy** or
orange-flavoured liqueur
(optional)

2 tablespoons **apricot jam**

100 g (3½ oz) **ground
hazelnuts** or **almonds**

50 g (2 oz) **caster sugar**

250 g (8 oz) **icing sugar**, plus
extra for dusting

yellow food colouring

1 tablespoon **egg white**

4–5 teaspoons **cold water**

25 g (1 oz) **green ready-to-
roll icing**

25 g (1 oz) **red ready-to-
roll icing**

Mini Christmas cakes

1 Drizzle the fairy cakes with the liqueur, if using. Spread $1/2$ teaspoon jam on to the centre of each cake.

2 To make the marzipan, put the ground nuts, caster sugar, 50 g (2 oz) of the icing sugar and a few drops of yellow food colouring in a bowl. Add the egg white and mix with a round-bladed knife until the mixture starts to cling together. Finish mixing the paste by hand until smooth and very firm. Lightly knead the marzipan and shape into a thick sausage, 7.5 cm (3½ inches) long. Cut into 12 thin slices and place a slice on top of each cake.

3 Put the remaining icing sugar in a bowl and add the cold water to make a thick smooth paste – the icing should hold its shape but not feel too firm. Gently spread the icing over the marzipan.

4 Use the green and red ready-to-roll icing to make small holly leaves and berries. Use to decorate the tops of the cakes.

Makes 12
Decoration time: 30 minutes

Love hearts

Make these as a family treat for Valentine's Day. Use Cream Cheese Frosting (see page 13) or White Chocolate Fudge Frosting (see page 14) instead of the glacé icing if preferred.

200 g (7 oz) **icing sugar**

4–5 teaspoons **rosewater** or **lemon juice**

12 **fairy cakes** (see pages 10–12)

100 g (3½ oz) **red ready-to-roll icing**

icing sugar, for dusting

6 tablespoons **strawberry jam**

1 Put the icing sugar in a bowl and add 4 teaspoons of the rosewater or lemon juice. Mix until smooth, adding a little more liquid if necessary, until the icing is a thick paste. Spread over the tops of the fairy cakes.

2 Knead the red ready-to-roll icing on a surface lightly dusted with icing sugar. Roll out thickly and cut out 12 heart shapes using a small heart-shaped cookie cutter. Place a heart on the top of each cake.

3 Press the jam through a small sieve to remove any seeds or pulp. Put the sieved jam in a small piping bag fitted with a writing nozzle. Pipe small dots into the icing around the edges of each cake and pipe a line of jam around the edges of the heart.

Makes 12
Decoration time: 20 minutes

12 **Vanilla Fairy Cakes**
(see page 10)

4 tablespoons **sherry** or
orange-flavoured liqueur
(optional)

200 g (7 oz) **icing sugar**,
sifted

1–2 tablespoons **lemon juice**

36 **sugared almonds**

12 **frosted flowers** (see
page 43)

fine white **ribbon**, to decorate

Wedding cupcakes

Prettily decorated with sugared almonds, these little cakes are perfect for a country-style family wedding. You could add guests' name tags to them and place them around the dining table. Choose sugared almonds to suit the colour scheme of the wedding. If using ribbon, secure it around the paper cases before you begin decorating.

1 Drizzle the cakes with the liqueur, if using. Mix the icing sugar in a bowl with 1 tablespoon of the lemon juice. Gradually add the remaining lemon juice, stirring well with a wooden spoon until the icing holds its shape but is not difficult to spread – you might not need all the juice.

2 Spread the lemon-flavoured icing over the tops of the fairy cakes using a small palette knife and arrange 3 sugared almonds in the centre of each.

3 Place a frosted flower on top of each cake and tie a length of white ribbon around each paper cake case to decorate it, finishing it with a bow.

Makes 12
Decoration time: 20 minutes

1 quantity **Chocolate Buttercream** (see page 13) or **Chocolate Fudge Frosting** (see page 14)

12 **Chocolate Fairy Cakes** (see page 10)

200 g (7 oz) **flaked chocolate bars**, cut into 2.5 cm (1 inch) lengths

36 candy-covered **chocolate mini eggs**

Easter nests

1 Using a small palette knife, spread the buttercream or chocolate icing over the tops of the fairy cakes, spreading the mixture right to the edges.

2 Cut the short lengths of flaked chocolate bars lengthways into thin 'shards'.

3 Arrange the chocolate shards around the edges of the cakes, pressing them into the icing at different angles to resemble birds' nests. Pile 3 eggs into the centre of each 'nest'.

Makes 12

Decoration time: 20 minutes

1 quantity **Buttercream** (see page 13)

yellow and **blue food colourings**

12 **fairy cakes** (see pages 10–12)

2 **glacé cherries**

Ducks, bunnies and chicks

1 Put two-thirds of the buttercream in a bowl, beat in a few drops of yellow food colouring and mix well. Using a small palette knife, spread the yellow icing in a flat layer over the tops of the fairy cakes.

2 Colour the remaining buttercream with blue food colouring. Place in a piping bag fitted with a writing nozzle, or use a greaseproof paper piping bag with the tip snipped off.

3 Pipe simple duck, bunny and chick shapes on to the iced cakes. Cut the glacé cherries into thin slices, then into tiny triangles and use to represent beaks on the ducks and chicks, and tiny eyes on the bunnies.

Makes 12
Decoration time: 25 minutes

300 g (10 oz) **icing sugar**

2 tablespoons **cold water**

black and **red food colourings**

12 **fairy cakes** (see pages 10–12)

12 **jelly insect sweets**

Spiders' webs

For best results, finish decorating one cake before moving on to the next as the icing must be really soft to make the web patterns work well. Use any selection of sweet insects – either the spiders or the bugs can be caught in the web!

1 Beat the icing sugar in a bowl with the cold water until smooth – the icing should be soft enough to lose its shape when the spoon is lifted from the bowl. If necessary add a dash more water.

2 Transfer one-quarter of the icing to a separate bowl and stir in a little black food colouring. Put in a piping bag fitted with a writing nozzle.

3 Colour the remaining icing red. Drop 1 teaspoonful of the red icing on to a cake and spread it to the edges. Starting at the edges of the cake, pipe a spiral of black icing that finishes in the centre of the cake. Run the tip of a cocktail stick or fine skewer from the centre of the spiral out to the edge. Repeat at intervals around the cake to make a spider's web pattern, then decorate with a jelly insect.

4 Repeat on all the remaining fairy cakes.

Makes 12
Decoration time: 25 minutes

Flying bats

125 g (4 oz) **black ready-to-roll icing**

icing sugar, for dusting

2 tablespoons **clear honey**

12 **fairy cakes** (see pages 10–12)

175 g (6 oz) **orange ready-to-roll icing**

1 tube **black writing icing**

selection of tiny red, orange and yellow **sweets**

1 Knead the black ready-to-roll icing on a surface lightly dusted with icing sugar. Roll out thickly and cut out 12 bat shapes by hand or using a small bat-shaped cookie cutter. Transfer to a baking sheet lined with nonstick baking parchment and leave to harden while decorating the cakes.

2 Spread ½ teaspoon honey over the top of each fairy cake. Thinly roll out the orange ready-to-roll icing and cut out circles using a 6 cm (2½ inch) round cookie cutter. Place an orange circle on top of each cake.

3 Place a bat on top of each cake. Dampen the edge of the orange icing and press the sweets gently into the icing. Pipe a wiggly line of black icing over the sweets.

Makes 12
Decoration time: 30 minutes

12 **Vanilla Fairy Cakes**
(see page 10)

1 quantity **Buttercream**
(see page 13)

Butterfly cakes

1 Using a small, sharp knife cut out the centre from each cake and slice each scooped-out piece in half.

2 Put the buttercream in a big piping bag fitted with a large star nozzle. Pipe a large swirl of icing into the hollow of each cake.

3 Reposition the cut-out centres on each cake at an angle of 45° so they resemble butterfly wings.

Makes 12
Decoration time: 15 minutes

7 tablespoons **raspberry** or **strawberry jam**

12 **Orange Fairy Cakes** (see page 10)

300 g (10 oz) **icing sugar**

2 tablespoons **orange juice**

Feather cakes

For these delicately patterned cakes, finish decorating one cake before starting on another as the icing quickly starts to set once spooned on to the cakes.

1 Press the jam through a sieve to remove any seeds or pulp. Put 3 tablespoons of the sieved jam into a small piping bag fitted with a writing nozzle and set aside. Spread the remaining jam over the tops of the fairy cakes.

2 Put the icing sugar in a bowl and beat in the orange juice until smooth – the icing should be soft enough to lose its shape when the spoon is lifted from the bowl. If necessary add a few more drops of juice.

3 Spoon a thick layer of icing on to a cake and spread it to the edges. Using the jam in the piping bag, pile large dots of jam, 1 cm (½ inch) apart, on to the icing in a spiral, working from the edge of the cake to the centre. Draw the tip of a cocktail stick or fine skewer through the dots so they almost join up.

4 Repeat on the remaining cakes and leave to set.

Makes 12
Decoration time: 15 minutes

Frosted primrose cakes

These make a great gift for Mum – on Mother's Day or at any time during spring when flowers like primroses are at their best. Once frosted, the flowers keep for several weeks in a cool place so you can make them well in advance.

1 Make sure the flowers are clean and thoroughly dry before frosting. Put the egg white in a small bowl and the sugar in another.

2 Using your fingers or a soft brush, coat all the petals on both sides with egg white. Dust plenty of sugar over the flowers until evenly coated. Transfer to a sheet of nonstick baking parchment and leave for at least 1 hour until firm.

3 Using a small palette knife, spread the chocolate frosting over the tops of the cakes. Decorate the top of each with the frosted flowers. Tie a length of ribbon around each paper cake case to decorate and finish in a bow.

Makes 12

Decoration time: 30 minutes

selection of small **spring flowers** such as primroses, violets or rose petals

a little lightly beaten **egg white**

caster sugar, for dusting

1 quantity **White Chocolate Fudge Frosting** (see page 14)

12 **Vanilla Fairy Cakes** (see page 10)

fine pastel-coloured **ribbon**, to decorate

200 g (7 oz) **icing sugar**, plus
a little extra

1–2 tablespoons **lemon** or
orange juice

12 **fairy cakes** (see
pages 10–12)

½ quantity **Buttercream** (see
page 13)

pink and **lilac food colourings**

Piped shell cakes

**These are great fun for all the family to create – children love piping
their own designs and personalizing cakes with names or messages.
The pink and lilac piping looks pretty on the white background but you
can choose any mixture of colours you like.**

1 Mix the icing sugar in a bowl
with 1 tablespoon of the lemon or
orange juice. Gradually add the
remaining juice, stirring well with
a wooden spoon until the icing
holds its shape but is not difficult
to spread. You might not need all
the juice.

2 Reserve 3 tablespoons of the
icing and spread the remainder
over the tops of the fairy cakes
using a small palette knife. Stir a
little extra icing sugar into the
reserved icing to thicken it until it
just forms peaks when lifted with a
knife. Put in a piping bag fitted
with a writing nozzle.

3 Colour half the buttercream with
pink food colouring and the other
half with lilac. Place in separate
piping bags fitted with star nozzles.

4 Pipe rows of pink, lilac and white
icing across some of the cakes.

Makes 12
Decoration time: 30 minutes

1 quantity **Cream Cheese Frosting** (see page 13) or **Buttercream** (see page 13)

12 **fairy cakes** (see pages 10–12)

selection of **small sweets**, such as mini mallows, gumdrops or jelly beans

Candy cakes

To make these cakes really effective stick to the same shades of colour throughout for the sweet decorations – either pastels or shocking colours – combining 2 or 3 different types of sweets. These are great fun for children to decorate.

1 Using a small palette knife, spread the frosting or buttercream over the tops of the fairy cakes.

2 Decorate each cake by sprinkling with a thick, even layer of small sweets.

Makes 12
Decoration time: 10 minutes

Stars, spots and stripes

1 Using a small palette knife, spread the buttercream in a thin layer over the tops of the cakes.

2 Knead the ready-to-roll icings on a surface lightly dusted with icing sugar, keeping the colours separate. Take 50 g (2 oz) of the white icing, roll out thinly and cut out 4 circles using a 6 cm (2½ inch) round cookie cutter. Cut out 6 small stars from each circle using a tiny star-shaped cutter. Thinly roll out a little of the blue icing and cut out stars. Fit the blue stars into each white round and carefully transfer to 4 of the cakes.

3 Thinly roll out another 50 g (2 oz) of the white icing. Roll balls of blue icing, about the size of a small pea, between the finger and thumb. Press at intervals on to the white icing. Gently roll with a rolling pin so the blue icing forms dots over the white. Cut out 4 circles using the round cookie cutter and transfer to 4 more of the cakes.

4 From the remaining blue and white icing cut out long strips 5 mm (¼ inch) wide and lay them together on the work surface to make stripes. Roll lightly with a rolling pin to flatten them and secure together, then cut out 4 more circles. Place on top of the remaining 4 cakes.

Makes 12
Decoration time: 20 minutes

½ quantity **Buttercream** (see page 13)

12 **fairy cakes** (see pages 10–12)

150 g (5 oz) **white ready-to-roll icing**

125 g (4 oz) **blue ready-to-roll icing**

icing sugar, for dusting

200 g (7 oz) (about ½ can) **sweetened condensed milk**

50 g (2 oz) **caster sugar**

65 g (2½ oz) **unsalted butter**

2 tablespoons **golden syrup**

12 **fairy cakes** (see pages 10–12)

100 g (3½ oz) **plain chocolate**, chopped

100 g (3½ oz) **milk chocolate**, chopped

Chocolate toffee cupcakes

1 Put the condensed milk, sugar, butter and golden syrup in a medium heavy-based saucepan and heat gently, stirring, until the sugar dissolves. Cook over a gentle heat, stirring, for about 5 minutes until the mixture has turned a pale fudge colour.

2 Leave to cool for 2 minutes then spoon the toffee over the top of the fairy cakes.

3 Melt the plain and milk chocolate in separate heatproof bowls, either one at a time in the microwave or by resting each bowl over a saucepan of gently simmering water. Place a couple of teaspoons of each type of melted chocolate on to a cake, mixing up the colours and tap the cake on the work surface to level the chocolate.

4 Using the tip of a cocktail stick or fine skewer, swirl the chocolates together to marble them lightly. Repeat on the remaining cakes.

Makes 12
Cooking time: 5 minutes
Decoration time: 15 minutes

50 g (2 oz) **unsalted butter**

50 g (2 oz) **caster sugar**

2 tablespoons **golden syrup**

100 g (3½ oz) **crispy rice breakfast cereal**

12 **fairy cakes** (see pages 10–12)

icing sugar, for dusting

Toffee crisp pyramids

1 Put the butter, sugar and golden syrup in a medium heavy-based saucepan and heat gently until the sugar dissolves. Cook the mixture for 2–3 minutes until it is pale toffee coloured, stirring frequently. Immerse the base of the pan in cold water to prevent further cooking.

2 Stir in the crispy rice breakfast cereal and mix until evenly coated. Pile a little of the mixture on to the top of each fairy cake and shape into a pyramid. Leave until cold then lightly dust the tops with icing sugar.

Makes 12

Cooking time: 5 minutes

Decoration time: 10 minutes

Tee-off cakes

Golf-crazy Dads will love these little fairy cakes, particularly if you get the children involved with the decoration. If you cannot find chocolate 'golf balls', you can easily shape some out of white ready-to-roll icing and make the golf ball-like impressions with the tip of a blunt-ended paintbrush.

1 Beat the chocolate spread or icing to soften it slightly then spread it over the tops of the fairy cakes using a small palette knife.

2 Knead the green ready-to-roll icing on a surface lightly dusted with icing sugar. Roll out thinly and cut out 12 circles using a 5 cm (2 inch) round cookie cutter. Place a green circle on top of each cake.

3 Use the white ready-to-roll icing to shape 12 small golf tees. Lay one on top of each cake, securing with a dampened paintbrush. Press a foil-wrapped chocolate golf ball into the icing, alongside the tee, to finish.

Makes 12
Decoration time: 30 minutes

8 tablespoons **chocolate hazelnut spread** or ½ quantity **Chocolate Fudge Frosting** (see page 14)

12 **fairy cakes** (see pages 10–12)

200 g (7 oz) **green ready-to-roll icing**

icing sugar, for dusting

75 g (3 oz) **white ready-to-roll icing**

12 **foil-wrapped chocolate golf balls**

12 **Vanilla Fairy Cakes**
(see page 10)

300 g (10 oz) small
strawberries

150 ml (¼ pint) **double cream**

2 teaspoons **caster sugar**

½ teaspoon **vanilla extract**

4 tablespoons **redcurrant jelly**

1 tablespoon **water**

Strawberry cream cakes

1 Using a small sharp knife, scoop out the centre of each fairy cake to leave each cake with a deep cavity. Reserve 6 of the smallest strawberries and thinly slice the remainder.

2 Using a hand-held electric whisk, whip the cream with the sugar and vanilla extract until just peaking. Spoon a little into the centre of each cake and flatten slightly with the back of the spoon.

3 Arrange the sliced strawberries, overlapping, around the edges of each cake. Halve the reserved strawberries and place a strawberry half in the centre of each cake.

4 Heat the redcurrant jelly in a small heavy-based saucepan with the water until melted, then brush over the strawberries using a pastry brush. Store the cakes in a cool place until ready to serve.

Makes 12
Decoration time: 20 minutes

3 small **oranges**

100 g (3½ oz) **caster sugar**

300 ml (½ pint) **water**

12 **Citrus Fairy Cakes** (see page 10)

Candied orange cupcakes

This recipe uses whole orange slices, including the skins. Cooked in syrup over a very low heat, they turn meltingly soft and delicious.

1 Slice the oranges as thinly as possible and discard any pips. Put the sugar in a medium heavy-based saucepan with the water and heat very gently, stirring with a wooden spoon, until the sugar dissolves.

2 Add the orange slices and reduce the heat to its lowest setting. Cover the saucepan and cook very gently for about 50–60 minutes or until the orange slices are thoroughly tender.

3 Transfer the slices to a plate using a slotted spoon and leave to cool slightly. Boil the syrup left in the saucepan until it is very thick and syrupy. Leave to cool for 5 minutes.

4 Arrange the orange slices over the fairy cakes. Brush the thickened syrup over the cakes and leave to cool completely.

Makes 12
Cooking time: 50–60 minutes
Decoration time: 10 minutes

Praline custard cakes

When making the caramel for these cakes, watch the saucepan closely towards the end of the cooking time. You want the caramel to be deep golden in colour but not too dark as the sugar will start to burn and taste bitter.

1 To make the caramel, put the sugar in a small heavy-based saucepan with the water. Heat gently, stirring with a wooden spoon, until the sugar has dissolved. Bring to the boil and boil rapidly for about 10 minutes, until the syrup has turned a golden caramel.

2 Immediately remove the pan from the heat and immerse the base in cold water for a few seconds to prevent further cooking. Stir in the nuts and tip the mixture on to a lightly oiled large baking sheet, spreading it in a thin layer. Leave for about 20 minutes until brittle.

3 Scoop out and discard the centre from each fairy cake using a teaspoon. Break the nut brittle in half and place one half in a polythene bag. Tap gently with a rolling pin until the brittle is broken into small chunks. Turn out on to a plate then put the remaining brittle in the bag. Beat firmly with the rolling pin until the brittle is finely crushed.

4 Mix the crushed brittle with the custard and pile the mixture into the cakes. Decorate with the large pieces of brittle.

Makes 12
Cooking time: 10 minutes, plus cooling
Decoration time: 15 minutes

100 g (3½ oz) **caster sugar**

100 ml (3½ fl oz) **water**

50 g (2 oz) **unblanched hazelnuts**, chopped

12 **Vanilla Fairy Cakes** (see page 10)

300 ml (½ pint) good-quality **creamy custard**

75 g (3 oz) **flaked almonds**

50 g (2 oz) **sultanas**

125 g (4 oz) **glacé cherries**, quartered

4 tablespoons **golden syrup**

12 **fairy cakes** (see pages 10–12)

50 g (2 oz) **plain chocolate**, broken into pieces

Florentine fairy cakes

1 Mix together the flaked almonds, sultanas, glacé cherries and golden syrup in a bowl. Tip the mixture out on to a greased baking sheet and spread in a thin layer. Bake in a preheated oven, 200°C (400°F), Gas Mark 6, for 8 minutes or until the nuts and syrup are turning golden. Remove from the oven and leave to cool slightly.

2 Break up the mixture and scatter over the cakes in an even layer.

3 Melt the chocolate in a heatproof bowl, either in the microwave or by resting the bowl over a saucepan of gently simmering water. Put the melted chocolate in a piping bag fitted with a writing nozzle. Scribble lines of chocolate across the fruit and nut topping. Leave to set.

Makes 12
Cooking time: 8 minutes
Decoration time: 10 minutes

12 **Coffee Fairy Cakes**
(see page 10)

4 tablespoons **coffee-flavoured liqueur**

300 ml (½ pint) **double cream**

75 g (3 oz) piece of **plain** or **milk chocolate**

cocoa or **drinking chocolate powder**, for sprinkling

Espresso cream cakes

These richly flavoured cakes make a delicious treat with morning coffee. If you don't want to use the liqueur, use 4 tablespoons of strong black coffee mixed with 1 teaspoon of sugar instead.

1 Flavour the fairy cakes by drizzling with 2 tablespoons of the coffee liqueur.

2 Put the remaining liqueur in a bowl with the cream and whip with a hand-held electric whisk until the cream is thickened and only just holds its shape. Using a small palette knife, spread the cream over the tops of the fairy cakes, swirling it right to the edges.

3 Using a vegetable peeler, pare off curls from the chocolate bar – if the chocolate breaks off in small, brittle shards, try softening it in the microwave for a few seconds first, but take care not to overheat and melt it. Scatter the chocolate curls over the cakes and sprinkle with a little cocoa or drinking chocolate powder. Store the cakes in a cool place until ready to serve.

Makes 12
Decoration time: 10 minutes

Chocolate truffle cakes

1 Coarsely grate 50 g (2 oz) of the chocolate and set aside. Chop the remainder into pieces.

2 Heat the cream in a small heavy-based saucepan until just beginning to bubble around the edges. Remove from the heat and add the chopped chocolate. Leave to stand for a few minutes until the chocolate has melted.

3 Turn the mixture into a bowl and leave to cool until the cream just holds its shape – you can pop it in the refrigerator for a short while but don't leave it for too long as the mixture will eventually set.

4 Using a small palette knife, spread the chocolate cream over the tops of the fairy cakes. Scatter the truffle quarters over the cakes. Sprinkle with the grated chocolate and leave the cakes in a cool place until ready to serve.

Makes 12
Decoration time: 15 minutes

200 g (7 oz) **plain chocolate**

150 ml (¼ pint) **double cream**

12 **Chocolate Fairy Cakes** (see page 10)

24 **cocoa-dusted chocolate truffles**, quartered

100 g (3½ oz) chunky piece of **white chocolate**

1 quantity **White Chocolate Fudge Frosting** (see page 14)

12 **White Chocolate Chip Fairy Cakes** (see page 10)

icing sugar, for dusting

White chocolate curl cakes

1 Using a vegetable peeler, pare off curls from the chocolate bar – if the chocolate breaks off in small, brittle shards, try softening it in the microwave for a few seconds first, but take care not to overheat and melt it. Set the chocolate curls aside in a cool place while icing the cakes.

2 Using a small palette knife, spread the fudge frosting all over the tops of the fairy cakes.

3 Pile the chocolate curls on to the fairy cakes and lightly dust with icing sugar.

Makes 12
Decoration time: 15 minutes

100 g (3½ oz) **white chocolate**, chopped

100 g (3½ oz) **milk chocolate**, chopped

100 g (3½ oz) **plain chocolate**, chopped

40 g (1½ oz) **unsalted butter**

12 **Chocolate Fairy Cakes** (see page 10)

cocoa powder, for dusting

Triple chocolate cupcakes

1 Put the white, milk and plain chocolate in separate bowls and add 15 g (½ oz) butter to each. Melt all the chocolate, either one at a time in the microwave or by resting each bowl over a saucepan of gently simmering water. Stir occasionally until melted and smooth.

2 Using a small palette knife, spread the melted white chocolate over 4 of the cakes and sprinkle with a little cocoa powder.

3 Put 2 tablespoons of the melted milk and plain chocolate in separate piping bags fitted with writing nozzles. Spread the milk chocolate over 4 more of the cakes and pipe dots of plain chocolate over the milk chocolate.

4 Spread the plain chocolate over the 4 remaining cakes and scribble with lines of piped milk chocolate.

Makes 12
Decoration time: 20 minutes

Index

Executive Editor Sarah Ford
Managing Editor Clare Churly
Executive Art Editor Geoff Fennell
Photographer Gareth Sambidge
Food Stylist Joanna Farrow